God, Was I Wrong?

Discover Hope and Healing Beyond Disappointment
About "The One" God Revealed As Your Future Spouse

LORI-KAYE MYLES

DAYELight
PUBLISHERS

ISBN: 978-1-966723-27-1 (paperback)

Dedicated to anyone experiencing immense hurt and struggling with their faith after facing disappointment about "the one" they believe God has revealed as their future spouse.

Foreword

I am truly honored to introduce Lori-Kaye's remarkable book, a courageous and vulnerable account of her personal journey. In it, she explores the complexities of relationships, faith, and personal growth.

When I met Lori-Kaye, she was reserved and trying her best to navigate a new space with new people. As I got to know her better, I discovered that she had faced a profound personal experience. This experience had left her questioning her faith and her understanding of God's plan— a story I could relate to, to some degree.

With unflinching honesty, she shares in her book her struggles to reconcile her expectations and faith with the reality of her experiences. As someone who has walked alongside Lori-Kaye, I can attest to the transformative power of her story. Her insights and reflections offer a beacon of hope for anyone who has faced disappointment, disillusionment, or uncertainty. Furthermore, the practical tips, scriptures quoted, and guided reflections are certainly an exceptional addition to this book, leaving you encouraged and empowered to restore your hope in the Lord.

I wholeheartedly endorse this book, and I am confident that it will resonate deeply with readers. Lori-Kaye's writing is infused with a sense of vulnerability, empathy, and compassion, making this book a precious resource for anyone seeking to navigate the complexities of disappointment in relationships and faith. I strongly recommend reading this superbly written book, which will give you insight into relationships and how to navigate when you believe God says yes, but it doesn't fall in line.

I pray that as you make your way all the way to the end of these pages, you will experience healing just like Lori-Kaye did.

—Danielle Grant

Acknowledgments

I would like to extend my sincerest gratitude to everyone who has contributed to the creation of this book in any way.

To my heavenly Father, words cannot describe the gratitude in my heart for Your inspiration to write this book. You are the backbone to my livelihood, and I give You honor for being constant in every moment of my life and for doing more than I could ever ask or think.

To my family, your unwavering support, love, and encouragement have been the bedrock of my journey. Mommy, your sacrifices for me have not gone unnoticed. Both you and Daddy play an instrumental role in the person and the author I am today. Uncle Travis, my role model, thank you for your assistance and effective feedback in making this dream a reality. To Grandma and Aunty Collette, your support has tremendously impacted my life. To all my close relatives, thank you for the ways you have impacted my life and this book.

To my friends, your prayers, advice, and enthusiasm have been a constant source of inspiration and support for me. Your willingness to listen, offer words of encouragement, and provide constructive feedback has been invaluable. To my discipleship sisters and work colleagues, thank you for being a vital part of my support system.

To my book launch team, your hard work and dedication during this time have helped me more than you would ever know. Thank you for seeing my vision and for your assistance in getting things ready.

To my book coach and publisher, Crystal Daye, you are the best book coach ever! Your expertise has been instrumental in bringing this book to life. Your team is the best!

And to everyone who has supported me along the way, your kindness, encouragement, and support have made a significant difference in my life and in the creation of this book. I'm honored to have you all in my corner, and I look forward to sharing this book with you.

To my reader, I am honoured that you decided to read this book. I hope that the words in this book will contribute to your restoration and a renewed hope in God. Thank you for supporting and purchasing my book.

Table of Contents

Introduction

It took me a few months to share with my closest friends and family what had happened. Months had passed before most people knew that we were no longer in a relationship. I was so hurt and confused that I did not know what to say to them or how to ask for support. Instead, I was trying to hold everything together and figure it all out.

I had been so sure, so convinced, that God had revealed my future husband to me. The confirmations, the signs, the feelings—everything pointed to it being the right choice. But in the aftermath of heartbreak and disappointment, I was left wondering if I had gotten it all wrong. I desired support, but I was too ashamed. How would I explain that the relationship with the person God revealed as "the one" ended, without looking like I did not know God's voice all this time or like a fool?

For the first part of this journey, I suffered in silence, and I don't want you to do the same. Instead, my desire is for you to receive the support, closure, and guidance you need as early as possible.

If you are reading this, chances are you are familiar with the pain of being wrong about "the one" God revealed to you.

Maybe you are in the midst of heartbreak or a broken engagement, questioning everything, including your faith. Maybe you are struggling to understand why God allowed this to happen to you. You are bombarded with endless questions: *"Was it all a lie? Did God mislead me? Why did this happen to me? How do I move forward? Is there hope?"*

You are not alone. I have been there too, and I'm here to tell you that there is hope. There is a way forward, a path to restoration and healing. In this book, we'll journey together through the process of making sense of what happened on a pathway to finding hope. We'll confront the questions and doubts that plague us when things don't go as planned. Furthermore, we'll explore biblical truths about relationships and God's character, and discover how to rebuild trust in God, even when our expectations are shattered.

This book is my story, but it is also your story. It is a story of redemption, hope, and restoration. So, let's begin.

Part A

Making Sense Out Of Nonsense

Chapter 1

Was It All A Lie?

It was 4 o'clock in the morning, and with swollen eyes and a whirlwind of pain in my chest, my mind was puzzled and filled with many questions. Not only was I exhausted from the non-stop crying, nausea, and heart palpitations, but also from a lack of sleep as I found it hard to fall and stay asleep. The sorrow and feelings of betrayal just would not allow me.

Was it all a lie? All this time?

I quickly ran to the bathroom, emptying my stomach as the overwhelming anxiety resulting in nausea took over. It was never supposed to be like this, not when you allow God to write your love story. He has plans to prosper me, not harm me, right? Then why was I confused and in so much pain and heartbreak after believing he showed me who my future husband was? My mind wandered back to better times and how it all started.

It was the summer right after high school graduation. I was finally an adult and about to start college. Seemingly, out of the blue, I got a request to connect on a very popular platform. *"Oh, I remember this guy, Bob,"* I said to myself as I accepted his request. *"I always saw him when the Christian club at my high school would meet up for fellowship with other schools."* A couple of hours later, he messaged me and I responded. We chatted a little, but he mentioned he was experiencing some issues with the platform, so he wanted to reach out on WhatsApp. *No big deal,* I figured. We would have had each other's numbers anyway before I changed phones.

Two weeks later, Bob and I were texting frequently, and by the following month, we met up in person and attended a gospel concert together. It was amazing! I could feel God's presence all around me. We were there praising and worshipping, and the gospel artiste said, *"Hold the hand of the person you are standing next to and pray for them."* We held each other's hands for the first time and prayed. *"As a matter of fact,"* said the gospel singer, *"Look at that person you are praying for and tell them you love them."* With our hands still together, I looked at him, and he looked at me. In the same breath, we said, *"I love you."* I felt something in my heart that night, a feeling of care and affection.

Time passed, and we eventually texted every day and would be on calls for hours, just talking and laughing. He would leave his college campus to come and visit me sometimes after my classes, and we would have a great time laughing,

16

talking about God, school and life, and just sharing corny jokes with each other. I've never felt so connected to someone else.

By October, he asked me to be his girlfriend. I was so happy! I felt joy in my heart and butterflies in my belly. That was something I had been praying to God about, and I received a revelation even before that: *he is my future husband.* I remember we were laughing and talking, and he was talking about how gorgeous my high school graduation picture was. He told me he would look at it often and admire how beautiful I was. Luckily for me, we were not face-to-face, or he would have seen the huge blush that glowed under my cheeks. After chatting and talking, there was a brief moment of stillness. He then asked me to be his girlfriend. At that moment, I said a quick prayer before responding. I felt a sense of confirmation, and I said yes! That night, I lay in my bed, smiling from ear to ear. I was now in a relationship— my first relationship! Plus, he loved God; ain't God good!

I smiled as I remembered that early in the summer, before we even reconnected, I had a desire for a relationship and to be in love. As our relationship continued, I received other confirmations, and I was just so grateful. By December, he met my family and spent a few days with them, and my mother absolutely loved him. By January, we were head over heels in love and already talking about marriage. Whenever he introduced me to someone significant, he would introduce me as his *"wife-to-be,"* even though we had only been together for several months and were not yet engaged. It was a fairytale come true, and we knew we had both found "the one." We studied together and did life side by side, looking forward to finishing college and saying, "I do."

But then…

"Crash!" was the sound of my heart when things didn't work out as expected. After being together for 3½ years, our relationship ended, and he was in another relationship within six weeks.

Ouch!

I was lost, confused, broken-hearted, angry, depressed, and felt close to the edge of a cliff. I had so many questions but no answers. I said to myself, *"I'm sure God revealed that he was my future husband. Was I wrong?"*

Does this resonate with you?

Perhaps God revealed to you who your future spouse is, but the relationship didn't work out. Or God showed you your future husband, but nothing has happened. You've been waiting for months, even years, but you've not become more than friends; or worse, you've never even spoken to each other before. Perhaps you've been waiting, but he pursued someone else and got married. Or possibly, both of you are considering marriage: the wedding date is set, and you've
18

bought the dress. You have moved and rearranged your life based on this divine revelation from God whom you trust, only to be left with the bitter taste of disappointment and a strong sense of heartbreak that could almost feel like a cardiac arrest.

My dear friend, you are not alone.

In addition to the heartbreak, doubt, and despair I was going through, I also felt a sense of aloneness. I felt like I could not talk about what I was going through. What do I do when someone asks me what's happening? Do I say, *"Oh, I'm facing immense despair as well as doubt in God because He revealed my future husband, but it didn't happen"?* No.

I was afraid of being laughed at, and I'm sure you are too. You might be scared of what others might have to say:

— *"That crazy girl, the one who is making stuff up in her head—she probably needs to get a mental check."*

— *"Oh, that fellow church sister who does not know God's voice? Does she even have a relationship with God?"*

— *"Yes, that girl. The one who told the church brother that God showed her he is her future husband and is now making him and his girlfriend uncomfortable.*

19

Didn't she know that they have been seriously dating?"

You may feel ashamed that you are the odd one out; that sheep that did not hear God's voice. Perhaps you know people who claim to have heard God's voice, and things have worked out for them or will work out for them. You might be saying to yourself, *"I was the only one who was made a fool out of this whole situation."*

You feel alone, don't you? As if no one understands the pain, frustration, and uncertainty. You feel as if you're the only one going through this because things seem to be working out for all other believers. I can assure you that you are not the only one going through this, which is definitely not meant to brush off what you are experiencing. Instead, it's to provide hope and support that it is possible to get through this.

You may be thinking, *"Was I living a lie? Was it all a lie?"* However, join me on this journey as we unravel and address your questions, concerns, hurt, and fear through this process of healing and rebuilding hope and trust in God.

Reflection

Grab your journal and write exactly how you are feeling at this moment.

Chapter 2

Who Is To Be Blamed?

Obviously God is to be blamed, right? Isn't He the one who led me down that path? He knows the future. He could have easily prevented it. As a matter of fact, He is the one who revealed to me that this person and I would get married.

I was so hurt and felt like God had disgraced me. All I could think was *"Why?"*

When I was about fifteen years old, I remember having this older friend who was a fervent believer. We were in the school chapel during lunchtime, as a group of us would frequently go there to pray, discuss the Bible, and just hang out. We were talking about relationships, and she said she prayed to the Lord and told Him she wanted His will in relationships. She essentially prayed that the first person she got into a relationship with would be her future husband. She prayed for God to prevent her from entering a relationship with anyone who wouldn't be her life partner, but to orchestrate things in such a way that her lifelong love would be her first love. I was in awe!

> "I couldn't wrap my mind around how a good God, who was supposed to be a source of light and guidance, led me down this very dark, lonely, and confusing road."

I was so in awe that I prayed the same prayer, hoping that the first person I would enter a relationship with would be my future husband. I prayed that God would guide me in such a way as to deter me from entering into a relationship with anyone who wasn't. So, when I met Bob, who became my first boyfriend, and things seemed to line up so well, it must have been God orchestrating everything.

Moreover, I would have prayed to God with a sincere heart to reveal if Bob was my future husband. I continued to present to God how I truly felt and continuously asked for clarity. I was sure I received confirmation. What made me even more certain is that when I questioned and doubted that Bob was "the one," scriptures about faith were laid on my heart, almost as if they were aiming to correct me of my unbelief. No wonder now that things didn't work out; the pain, hurt, and anger are so deep. The wound runs deep as the ocean because I trusted God, He directed me, and He apparently failed. This was why I blamed God.

I couldn't wrap my mind around how a good God, who was supposed to be a source of light and guidance, led me down this very dark, lonely, and confusing road.

"Why, Lord?" I would repeat over and over as if those were the only two words in English I knew. *"I prayed, and you gave me confirmations, so why?"* The sheet on my bed was damp from tears, and my pillow was stifling from the strong grip in my arms as I held it for comfort.

My mind, enveloped by despair and clouded with so many thoughts, drifted back to all the revelations and confirmations I received from God, both before entering a relationship with Bob and after.

Before we entered a relationship:

1. About a week and a half before reconnecting with Bob, I remember seeing a fellow Christian that I knew hanging out with her boyfriend on her verandah and wondering, *"When will that be me? When would God allow me to meet my special someone?"* I felt the Lord saying that I would meet someone very soon. Bob reached out the following week.

2. One Sunday evening, I was folding some clothes and listening to my favorite gospel playlist. As I folded the clothes, my mind wandered into a dreamy daze, and I pondered in my heart whether Bob was my

God-ordained spouse. So I asked for a sign. I was going to ask for a bee to fly. However, instead, the sign would be if Bob called me right as the song I was listening to ended, and just before the next song started. This was early in our friendship when we communicated via text messages and WhatsApp. Guess what? Bob called me just as the song I was listening to ended.

3. As I continued to ruminate (dreamily, I might add) on whether the Lord was really showing me that Bob would be my future husband through the signs I had received, I continued to question if this was truly the case. I started questioning everything and feeling some hints of doubt when I felt a scripture being laid on my heart: *"The Israelites did not enter the promised land because of unbelief."* I knew right then and there that God was telling me not to doubt, that I should not let unbelief turn me away from the promise He had revealed to me. Instead, I should have faith. I turned to my Bible, and there it was, Hebrews 3:19, the verse that confirmed for me that I should not doubt this promise and revelation from God, of who my future husband would be.

After we entered a relationship:

1. Several months into our relationship, I had a dream about a wedding. In the dream, I was the bride, and I was getting ready before walking down the aisle.

There were many people in the dream that I did not recognize. However, I did recognize Bob, and in the dream, he was the groom.

2. I met Bob's sister-in-law. Bob had a sister-in-law whom he was relatively close to, and her advice meant a great deal to him. At the beginning of our relationship, he said that he believed I was "the one" God had for him. However, he added that he would only know for certain if I met his sister-in-law in person. He had always prayed that one of the first people his future wife would meet and interact well with would be his sister-in-law, Mary. In previous relationships, even if his then-girlfriend was scheduled to meet Mary, it somehow didn't work out, and they never met. However, I met Mary. We spoke, laughed, and had great conversations.

3. We got engaged; after being together for 3½ years, he proposed.

As I sat amidst the shattered remains of our relationship, I couldn't shake the feeling that God had failed me. The hurt, confusion, and anger threatened to consume me. I could hardly even focus at work. My days were blurred together in a haze of tears and questions. I felt lost, alone, and abandoned. My prayers, once filled with conviction, assurance, and faith, now exude uncertainty.

After a few months of being demotivated to eat, sleep, bathe, or just live, I prayed, *"God, just give me strength to carry out basic functions and tasks."*

Even though I was uncertain about everything, I still tried to read my Bible and pray. My prayers, however, were more like me interrogating God and showing Him how much hurt had been caused. Moreover, I sought to find characters in the Bible who were also facing despair and going through a hard patch in life, as well as with their relationship with God. I just needed to see if I could find some relatability and comfort, just to prove that I was not "the only one."

Naomi's words were the exact thoughts in my mind, but phrased differently.

"Don't call me Naomi," she told them. *"Call me Mara, because the Almighty has made my life very bitter. I went away full, but the Lord has brought me back empty. Why call me Naomi?* **The Lord has afflicted me; the Almighty has brought misfortune upon me."** *(Ruth 1:20-21 – NIV – emphasis mine).*

Someone gets it, I thought to myself.

The scripture kept ringing in my ears, especially when Naomi said, *"The Lord has afflicted me; the Almighty has brought misfortune upon me."* This is exactly how I felt, and I'm sure that is how you might be feeling too.

Naomi, however, did have a plot twist; her devastated life turned into one that was blessed and full of joy. Everything she lost and the pain she went through were all overshadowed by the grace of God. It didn't happen overnight; however, through it all, Naomi was able to be honest about how she felt, and she journeyed to find her way back to hoping and trusting in God. And your story will be no different.

You will also have a plot twist of grace, joy, and restoration. Perhaps you can't even imagine that being a possibility right now, and that is okay. Nonetheless, you will look back one day in retrospect and see God's hands working out things for your good.

You may be thinking, *"The same God who misled me and caused me to be in this devastating situation in the first place? Isn't He to be blamed for this all?"*

Trust me, I get it. I couldn't help but also be upset with God for allowing this to happen in the first place. However, the more I blamed and questioned God, the more a little thought in the back of my mind said, *"But what if God is not the one to be blamed for all this mess?"*

I would shrug and dismiss that thought. However, time and time again, it would come up. *"What if, in truth and in fact, I contributed in some way or another to this mess and, in reality, should shoulder some of the blame?"*

Lori-Kaye Myles

I sat there and pondered.

I know it's hard for you to even entertain such questions, as they are comparable to throwing salt in your wounds. However, the fact of the matter is that sometimes, the process of healing a wound can be uncomfortable or even involve ointments that cause a temporary sting. Similarly to dressing a wound, your journey to healing and rebuilding trust in God will require moments of careful examination and possible "ointments that sting." Nevertheless, it is always better than leaving the wound unattended to fester and get worse.

> the process of healing a wound can be uncomfortable or even involve ointments that cause a temporary sting.

The question still remains: *Isn't God to be blamed for all this?*

Uncomfortable Questions

There is no doubt that I had about a million questions in my mind per minute about this whole situation. The questions I could not shake from the front of my mind was, *"Why did God even allow me to go through this? Why didn't He stop me when He realized that things were not going to work out?"*

But then, as I started to reflect, the uncomfortable question arose: *"What if God was also giving me warnings, but I was*

28

so love-struck and bent on this person being 'the one' that I was blind to them?"

Then I remembered something crucial. Bob and I would have broken up before. Two weeks before things officially ended, we broke up. However, we then got back together and tried to work things out. The truth is, my life felt like a huge chunk of it was missing without Bob in it. Nevertheless, after trying the relationship again, we broke up again.

> "What if God was also giving me warnings, but I was so love-struck and bent on this person being 'the one' that I was blind to them?"

So, upon reflecting again on the question, *"Why didn't God stop me if He realized things would end like this?"* I wondered if there was a possibility that if He had given me warnings, I would still have continued in the relationship.

"That is not possible!" I said to myself. *"If God had wanted to stop this whole situation before it got this bad, He would have. If He wanted to warn me that this relationship—that He led me to and promised—was not His will, He would have clearly stated that."*

A familiar, unquenchable pain in my chest quickly surfaced as thoughts raced through my mind. *"If God wanted to, He would have,"* I kept on repeating to myself. Deep down, there was a very uncomfortable question I did not want to address.

What if I was wrong all along?

"I couldn't have been wrong all this time and for so many years," I mumbled to myself, *"especially not when I received confirmations from God."*

I started crying uncontrollably as I remembered all the confirmations that I received from God and how things ended contrary instead.

My mind would frequently ponder the confirmations I received from the Lord. I was reminded that God speaks in many ways. He can speak to and direct us through His Word, dreams, other people, and even through how real circumstances unfold.

It took me about two years to process the entire situation that happened. The first several months involved me being confused, disappointed, heartbroken, and just trying to carry out basic daily tasks. The next several months were filled with me continuously questioning God, trying to create and maintain communication boundaries with Bob to help with my healing process, and trying to get the support and help I needed. Over the last several months, I have been rebuilding my trust and relationship with God and walking out my journey of healing and restoration.

Throughout the two years of processing everything and trying to rebuild my relationship with God, I was able to conduct some necessary examinations of my life, and I honestly realized that God was showing me other signs that I had ignored.

I found myself in a state of "confirmation bias." This is a tendency to search for, interpret, and recall information in a way that suits your pre-existing ideas and beliefs. I was so in love that I kept on looking only for confirmations throughout the entire relationship, despite whatever was going on.

As a result, there were some things that I ignored:

- When Bob and I were just communicating as friends, and I believed I had confirmation that he was my future husband, there was a strong prompting on my heart to fast from my phone. The Holy Spirit was guiding me to simply worship, pray, and read my Bible; to dwell in His presence. The first night I started, it was going okay until I checked my phone and saw some missed calls from Bob. At that moment, my phone rang, and I answered—in my defense—to just hear for a brief moment what Bob had to say since he had called so many times. We ended up talking for hours, and I neglected to read the Word and dwell in God's presence that night. At the time, I thought nothing of the whole situation.

31

However, looking back at that moment, I believe God wanted me to dwell in His presence and Word for a reason. Looking back, if I had followed through, the Lord might have given me more clarification during that time.

- Another time I believed I ignored God's guidance was the first time Bob visited me at my university campus. This occurred a few weeks before we officially started dating. We were texting as usual, and he said he wanted to visit me because it had been a while since we last saw each other. Even though I wanted to as well, I felt the Holy Spirit saying, *"Wait, not now."* I told him, *"Not now. I feel we should wait a bit before meeting up."* However, he kept saying how much he missed me and wanted to see me face-to-face again. Once again, I relented. We met up, and after that, things took off like a rocket, and our relationship went full speed ahead.

- I believe another way the Lord was trying to guide me was through my dreams. Do you remember the dream I mentioned earlier in the book as a confirmation? The one where we were getting ready on our wedding day? I was so focused on the part of the dream where it was our wedding day that I totally ignored all other proceedings. In the dream, yes, I was dressed in a wedding dress, and Bob was the groom. However, we did not get married in the dream; instead, things got put off. I don't remember all the details of the dream, but the outcome was that there was some major confusion. I was confused in the dream, and people around me were confused as well. Everyone in the dream was confused about why they were there and what was happening. I got this dream within the first three months of us being together. But I was so in love; I held tightly to the fact that in the dream, we were dressed in wedding attire. Maybe if I had even reflected and asked God for clarification, I would have gotten it.

- Lastly, I ignored practical things. God can guide us through practicality and how occurrences unfold. The fact of the matter is that, in all practicality, there were natural things I could have used to identify that Bob was not necessarily God's will for me. We had arguments every time we tried to discuss the Word of God. We could not agree. How can two walk unless they agree? (see Amos 3:3). We could not conduct a Bible study without having arguments—not disagreements, but arguments—about either the interpretation or application of the Word. This should have been an obvious sign to me that we were unequally yoked.

There are many other examples I could give of possible ways I ignored supernatural or practical guidance that would have helped me to make a better decision regarding the relationship. Nevertheless, I was just so eager to find "the one" that I only paid attention to anything that confirmed my *own* desires in my heart.

> God's guidance is often complex and nuanced, requiring us to trust in His sovereignty and wisdom.

As you sit in the midst of your shattered dreams and broken heart, it's natural to wonder if God has abandoned you. It's common to blame God, especially when you truly believe He led you down this path. You would have prayed for guidance and gotten signs and revelations. Perhaps it was prophesied that you would marry this person, or maybe even an elder confirmed this is the way to go. The pain and disappointment can be overwhelming, making it difficult to see a way forward, but it's in these moments of darkness that we are forced to confront our deepest fears and doubts.

The truth is that God's guidance is often complex and nuanced, requiring us to trust in His sovereignty and wisdom.

Reflection

- Were there any warning signs (spiritual, emotional, and/or practical) that you ignored or downplayed?

- Were there any instances of misinterpretation of signs and confirmations?

Chapter 3

The Questioning

Months would pass with me still having many questions and receiving few direct answers. One evening, as I found enough strength to clean my room, I stumbled upon my journal, which I had not used in a while, hidden beneath a pile of dusty books. Its pages, once filled with hopeful scribbles and prayer requests, now seemed like a cruel reminder of my disappointment.

I hesitated, then opened the journal, scanning the entries that chronicled various moments in my life. Tears streamed down my face. *"God, I don't understand. Why did You lead me here only to abandon me? Why did You let me trust in something that wasn't real?"*

My head started hurting from all the thoughts and questions running through my mind.

— *"Did God break His promise?*
— *"Did He mislead me?"*
— *"Was God truly good?*

— *"Had He failed me, or had I failed Him?"*

— *"Would I ever find love again?*

— *"Will I be alone forever since I lost 'the one'"?*

Some of these questions might be very similar to those you have as you navigate this whole process and situation of God revealing your future spouse, only for it not to come to pass. You might even be surprised by and feel ashamed of some of the questions that arise in your mind, especially those about God. However, be certain that you are not the first to have many questions about a situation. It is a natural part of disappointment and uncertainty. We see where Job had questions as he experienced devastation when he lost everything: his family, possessions, and health (see Job 10:1-3). We see where Jeremiah questioned God about justice and why the wicked prosper (see Jeremiah 12:1-4). We see where Habakkuk had questions for God about fairness and wrongdoing (see Habakkuk 1:2-4,13-17). Even the Psalmist had questions as he explored the various emotions he felt about the occurrences in his life (see Psalm 10:1-2, 22:1-2).

> You might even be surprised by and feel ashamed of some of the questions that arise in your mind, especially those about God.

So, my dear friend, don't condemn yourself for your moments and process of "questioning." God is not surprised by our questions when we are disappointed. There are even moments where He will clearly answer (see Habakkuk 1:5-11). However, during our period of questioning, much thought must be given to ensure that we remain humble and reverent as we are open and honest with God about our questions and feelings.

Let's dive into some of the major underlying factors using different scenarios from which most of our other questions come.

Questioning God's Goodness

You went to a conference, and a prophet saw you and said, *"Woman of God, get ready as the Lord is sending you your Boaz."* You marvel, as it was just last week that you read the book of Ruth and prayed that the Lord would grant you favor to find a man like Boaz. Six weeks later, you meet someone on social media who shares your love for God, and you connect so well in every area of life. After months of a long-distance relationship, you feel a strong desire to relocate. You prayed, and in a dream, you saw yourself on a plane. You may recall the book of Ruth and how Ruth was willing to relocate from her hometown to accompany Naomi. So, you decide to sell your vehicle and relocate to be closer to your Boaz. When you get there, things don't work out as imagined, and you return home five months later with a broken heart and less financially stable.

Lori-Kaye Myles

You are then left with the question: *"How could God be good when He allowed this?"*

Questioning God's Will And Plan

You heard God tell you who your future spouse would be four years ago. You walk by each other at church and speak briefly because you serve in ministry together. Longingly, you look for the day he will finally get the revelation from the Lord and pursue a relationship with you. However, two months ago, the pastor announced an engagement, and it's between your God-ordained spouse and another woman. You cried your eyes out, but still said, *"The Lord is faithful. This is just a test of my faith. I will still have faith in the promise. Soon enough, He will know I am the one for him and leave her. He and I will get married."* However, they came back from their honeymoon last week, and you can see videos of them on social media testifying to God's goodness and how He brought them together.

You are then left with the question: *"Was this truly God's will? Why did He let me wait for years, only to cause disgrace?*

Questioning God's Character

You have been praying for a husband for fifteen years, and you have seen many younger mentees around you get married before you do. You hold closely onto scriptures about God giving you the desires of your heart—ask and you

40

shall receive—and the Lord being able to do exceedingly above what you could ever ask. Yet still too many years have passed, and you have not gotten what you have asked for, much more exceedingly more than you could ask.

You are then left with the question: *"Is God faithful to His promises?"*

In life, it is often the natural response to have questions when things don't go as planned, hoped, or even promised. Based on our previous experiences or the experience of those around us that we have observed, we usually come up with an answer.

In order to answer normal and even practical things that happen in life, there are generally some natural laws to help us with a final answer. For example, you know that if a glass cup is placed on an unstable surface and wobbles, or if it slips out of your hand, it will fall and break.

> **"** Nevertheless, behind all of this is the natural law of gravity, which is constant and unchanging. **"**

If someone were to ask, *"How did the glass break?"* you would tell them that it fell or slipped from your hand.

Nevertheless, behind all of this is the natural law of gravity, which is constant and unchanging. If you let go of an object in your hand, it will fall. Whether now, or you unclenched it decades ago, or you plan to loosen your grip in the future, you know the object will fall because of the constant force of gravity.

Now, let us talk about the God of heaven and earth, the one who created everything, including natural laws such as gravity.

He is the same yesterday, today, and forever. (Hebrews 13:8 - ERV).

This may not be what you want to hear now in your state of agony and despair. And this is definitely not me slapping a band-aid on your massive wound or shoving your heart-wrenching questions and uncertainty under the carpet. No.

> **"**
> He is the same yesterday, today, and forever. (Hebrews 13:8 - ERV).
> **"**

Instead, this is an acknowledgment of a fundamental truth that will help pave your way forward to healing, restoration, and jubilation.

As an overthinking problem solver, I always ask why and come up with possible explanations for all the questions that arise in my mind. I questioned why God would allow this to happen and where He was in it all. How could He be good, and what happened to what He promised? However, in this case, I had no answer for why God allowed me to believe that someone was my spouse for 3.5 years, yet it not coming to pass. I had no answer for what would happen next in my life and how I would pick myself up again. I had no answer for how I would heal from the hurt.

Nonetheless, looking back, I can surely see God's hand in my life in the form of love, protection, and mercy. Now I see all the warning signs I ignored. Now I see how going through that period of mayhem helped me to introspect on some of the trauma that guided how I handled relationships in an unhealthy manner. Now I see how I made

> You probably won't have a clear-cut, simple answer to all the questions you have now, but what you do have are fundamental truths that will help you navigate it all.

marriage an idol above God. And now I see how what I experienced will be a testimony and catalyst for others to break free and heal.

"Life's challenges don't necessarily come with simple multiple-choice answers and explanations for a question or problem. Instead, it is mostly like an essay where you draw from the fundamental principles you know and apply them to the questions and problems at hand." —Lori-Kaye Myles

You probably won't have a clear-cut, simple answer to all the questions you have now, but what you do have are fundamental truths that will help you navigate it all.

God Is Good

According to the Merriam-Webster Dictionary, "good" means *"favourable in character, benevolent, right and commendable."* Thus, of a sound character and mean well with good intentions.

Growing up and attending church, I would always hear people say, *"God is good,"* which was always followed by the response, *"All the time."* I had grown accustomed to this so that it became an automated response from my lips whenever someone referred to God as good. However, in my time of devastation, the automation crashed. It was hard to say *"All the time,"* as during this time God did not appear to be good —well, towards me, at least. There are many things in life that I have experienced that are not good, and even many stories with outcomes far from good.

Once, I heard a story of someone who allowed his child to die. Yes, to die! He did not just allow it; he put things in place and did nothing about it, even though he could. The first word that comes to mind is *"Heartless."* Wouldn't you agree? I don't have a child yet, but when I do, I know I will do anything to ensure his/her safety.

But…God was good.

44

That illustration is really an overly simplified version of the gospel, specifically Jesus' death on the cross. At first glance, the above analogy appears to be a troubling one, suggesting a heartless father. However, in true understanding of the gospel, the analogy represents and shows a good God—one who loved humans so much that He gave His only Son to die on the cross. The fact of the matter is that God is naturally good, and He cannot be otherwise.

He created this earth and all that we need in it to carry out the normal functions of living things (such as respiration, reproduction, growth, and development). Even after the fall of mankind, He made a way through His Son to redeem us (see John 3:16-18). He allows us to receive sunlight and rain, whether we are righteous or unrighteous (see Matthew 5:45). Not to mention how we have air to breathe freely. Furthermore, I am sure there are several personal moments in your life when you experienced that God is good. For me, it was that night when my dad got some money earlier than expected and bought me a meal after all we ate earlier was rice because there was no more food in the house. It was that Sunday evening, while doing charity at a nearby elderly home, that I received a small package containing a bar of soap and food items. As a struggling college student with nothing to eat and no soap to take a bath that evening, this was a welcome gift that showed me God's goodness when I needed it most. Or it was that heartbroken girl who now sees how God's goodness has been evident in never leaving her side during this whole process, how He has turned it around for good, and has given her joy in place of mourning.

Does anything come to mind that reminds you that *God is good*?

Discrediting all the good things the Lord does because of a few situations would not be a reasonable deduction or conclusion. He is a good Father.

A parent may allow a baby learning to walk to stumble a little and get back up as she learns to walk, but that does not mean the parent does not care. Those moments of learning to walk are crucial to a baby's development. The parent is there holding onto the baby, catching her, and even guiding her steps as the baby learns to walk. This is also true of God; He is good and cares for us.

> Discrediting all the good things the Lord does because of a few situations would not be a reasonable deduction or conclusion. He is a good Father.

"The Lord is good to all; he has compassion on all he made." (Psalm 145:9 – NIV).

Yet hope returns when I remember this one thing: The Lord's unfailing love and mercy still continue, fresh as the morning, as sure as the sunrise. The Lord is all I have, and so in him I put my hope. (Lamentations 3:21-24 – GNT).

You are good, and what you do is good; teach me your decrees. (Psalm 119:68 – NIV).

Reflection

1. Write down honest questions about God and your situation that you might have. Repent for any presence of pride and irreverence.

2. Reflect on two previous things in your life that you couldn't understand and questioned God about for which you eventually got the answer or saw purpose in. How did you get the answer (maybe right away, years later, or still unraveling), and what was a key takeaway from those previous situations?

Chapter 4

God's Sovereignty and Human Choice in Finding a Spouse

My housemates used to call me "Ribs." Every time they said it, a big smile would come across my face, and I would blush. I was in a relationship that I believe God chose for me. I got the nickname "Ribs" because Bob and I believed I was his "missing rib." In Genesis, when God made Eve, he took a rib from Adam and used it to form Eve. So, Bob would call me his other "Rib." He—and eventually I—believed that every man has a missing rib, and when he meets her, he will somehow mystically know that this is his other half and soulmate.

What a faulty belief.

Growing up, I would always watch romantic movies and yearn to find my soulmate, my other half, the one who completes me. As I matured, this ideology deepened, as I gained experience hearing others say that they had met "the one."

Nevertheless, as believers, it is essential that we know we are not some "halves" walking around on earth, waiting to find another "half" to complete us and fulfill our purpose. We are made in God's image, and we are His handiwork. We are unique individuals, and we are made whole in Christ. We must be mindful that we don't walk around searching for a level of purpose, fullness, and wholeness in life from "my other half" that only Christ can give. Jesus is truly the one who makes us whole and completes our lives.

You may be in a season where you are still unsure about many things. You are trying to hold onto your faith in God; however, you still have many questions regarding dating, marriage, and finding a future spouse.

> we are not some "halves" walking around on earth, waiting to find another "half" to complete us and fulfill our purpose.

Now, I must say that in truth and in fact, I do not and will not have all the answers to all the questions you might have. I am still in the process of learning and studying God's Word. Nevertheless, what I do have and will share are some guiding principles from the Bible.

One of the biggest questions that might be on your heart is: *"Does God choose who a believer should marry, or does he/she have a choice?"*

In my opinion, this is a very complex question. Most people answer with a simple "Yes" or "No," which I believe I could provide in a one-word response. Nevertheless, I don't believe that would be sufficient.

To fully answer this question, I believe we must first explore the underlying factors of God's sovereignty and human free will.

Is God Sovereign? Yes.

All the peoples of the earth are regarded as nothing. He does as he pleases with the powers of heaven and the peoples of the earth. No one can hold back his hand or say to him: "What have you done?" (Daniel 4:35 – NIV).

which God will bring about in his own time—God, the blessed and only Ruler, the King of kings and Lord of lords. (1 Timothy 6:15 – NIV).

For from him and through him and for him are all things. To him be the glory forever! Amen. (Romans 11:36 – NIV).

According to Dictionary.com, the word "sovereign" as an adjective means *"having supreme rank, power and authority. Being above all others in character, importance, and excellence."* In addition to this, the word "sovereign" was frequently used in the past to represent a king or queen, someone who ruled over a people.

Do humans have free will/a choice? Yes.

But if serving the Lord seems undesirable to you, then choose for yourselves this day whom you will serve, whether the gods your ancestors served beyond the Euphrates, or the gods of the Amorites, in whose land you are living. But as for me and my household, we will serve the Lord." (Joshua 24:15 – NIV).

For God so loved the world that he gave his one and only Son, that whoever believes in him shall not perish but have eternal life. (John 3:16 – NIV).

The Spirit and the bride say, "Come!" And let the one who hears say, "Come!" Let the one who is thirsty come; and let the one who wishes take the free gift of the water of life. (Revelation 22:17 – NIV).

So, it is safe to say that in some instances, two things can be right at the same time. Another person described it as two sides of the same coin.

Now, how does this relate to finding a spouse?

God is sovereign, meaning He has supreme power and ruling over the earth and His creation. In addition to being sovereign, He is all-knowing and holy in character.

Although God is the supreme ruler, He does not necessarily decide and absolutely control every single action of humans.

Humans do have free will and a choice in what they do. Let me explain using an example to illustrate what I'm trying to say. God does not control and decide for someone if they brush their teeth or not today. That is a very basic and simple example; nevertheless, it explains what I am trying to convey regarding human choice.

Similarly to brushing our teeth, God allows us to make choices in other areas of our lives. For example: which school to attend, which job to take, who to choose as friends, and more. Nevertheless, as Christians, it is essential that in our free will and decision-making in all aspects of our lives, we include God. Furthermore, we should make decisions based on the godly and wise advice and commandments He has outlined in His Word.

Once again, you may ask: *How does this answer the question of relationships?*

Human Choice When Finding a Spouse

In relationships and marriage, God provides us with a choice. He does not necessarily dictate to you that this is the person you must marry. As previously mentioned, as followers of Christ, we make decisions based on what God says, which can primarily be found in His Word. So, yes, believers do get to choose who they marry, in accordance with God's Word and guidance.

Now, someone may say, *"God chose my spouse for me. He showed me who my future husband/wife was in a dream, and we are still married to this day."*

Okay, awesome. God was able to guide that individual through a dream to a fellow believer who would be a good match. God can guide us in many ways. It can be through His Word, dreams and prophecies, confirmations from other believers/elders, placing desires in our hearts, or even through practical circumstances.

In many ways, we can meet someone who could potentially seem like a good match for us. However, it is paramount that we pay attention to the fruit they bear and always look to God's Word for the characteristics to look out for. Don't get married to someone because you had a dream of them, and a prophet prophesied that the man you're wondering about is "the one." Ensure that the fruit this person produces aligns with the Word of God.

Don't go preparing to marry this person because of the prophetic revelations you have received, yet they are pushing you to fornicate, are abusive, or lack spiritual accountability and discipline. Once again, be governed by the characteristics and attributes described in the Word of what a godly person/spouse is like.

So, all in all, we do have a choice when it comes to relationships. In 1 Corinthians 7, Paul extensively discusses relationships. He speaks about singleness as well as
54

marriage and expounds on whether a believer *chooses* to pursue either. 1 Corinthians 7:39 encourages that a woman *"is free to marry anyone she wishes, but he must belong to the Lord"* after her husband dies. We do have a choice, whether we are single and this is our first husband, or we are widowed and this is not our first husband. Nevertheless, the key takeaway is that he should be a believer and that God should be in the midst of all our decision-making. God may speak to us through various ways, but we must be primarily guided by the truth and wisdom in God's Word when making choices.

Boaz chose to take Ruth as his wife, and David chose to request Abigail's hand in marriage, which she accepted.

Rebekah and Issac

I love the story of Rebekah and Isaac, and I believe it illustrates God's sovereignty and human free will in how these two individuals got married.

The story is found in Genesis 24, where Abraham is growing old and wants his son Isaac to get married. He did not want Issac to get married to any of the Canaanite women, so he told his servant to make an oath to find a wife from his (Abraham's) own country (see Genesis 24:3-4). Abraham *chose* where he wanted Isaac's wife to come from. The servant agreed but questioned what if the woman he found did not *choose* to come and marry Isaac; what then (see

Genesis 24:8). And Abraham advised that the servant would be free from the oath in that case.

Abraham's servant then heads out to find a wife for Isaac. He prays to God to find favour and asks for a sign that the woman he asks for a drink, who gives not just him but his camel water to drink as well, will be Isaac's wife (see Genesis 24:14). Here came Rebekah doing exactly what he asked for as a sign (see Genesis 24:17-20). Nevertheless, even after the confirmation of the sign, he *"watched her closely to learn whether or not the Lord made his journey successful" (Genesis 24:21 – NIV)*. In essence, he observed her and took note of how she operated and behaved. Thereafter, he requests to see her family and has a conversation with her brother and household, telling them of all that has happened and that he was there to find a wife for Isaac (see Genesis 24:28-48). Rebekah's brother then agreed that this must be the work of God, and agreed that Rebekah could be taken as Isaac's wife (see Genesis 24:51). Nevertheless, after all of that, they asked Rebekah for her input and what her choice would be if she were to go with this man. She said, *"I will go"* (see Genesis 24:57-58). Rebekah was then brought back to Isaac, where the servant recounted to him all that had happened. Isaac, after hearing everything, chose to marry her.

I believe this is a beautiful story that we can learn a great deal from.

God's sovereignty and our free will both play a part in who we will marry in the future. Moreover, if you believe you made a decision that was not the best in the whole process, God is so sovereign that He is able to bring about restoration and carry out His ultimate will, regardless. His ultimate will included us having fellowship with Him, and even though Adam and Eve's decision led to sin, which broke that fellowship and connection, God's ultimate will for us to have fellowship with Him is happening through salvation through Christ.

I am saying all of this to say that God is sovereign, and we can trust in His Word and His character as we choose and make decisions for the future.

Reflection

1. What are your current thoughts as it relates to God's sovereignty and human free will?

2. Contemplate and write if there were any moments in your life (outside of relationships) where you saw both God's sovereignty and human free will working hand in hand in a situation.

Part B

Restoration by F.A.I.T.H.

Chapter 5

Fight the Lies

The enemy's aim is to devour you, but you have overcome through Christ Jesus, and the truth sets you free.

The journey towards healing and restoration can be challenging, especially given the severity of the hurt and wound.

After going through the initial phase of chaotic thoughts, depression, questioning God, and just bawling my eyes out, I started improving and adjusting back to my normal self. Nonetheless, moments would come where the trauma resurfaced, and I would doubt any progress made and be tempted to give up.

> The fact of the matter is that in your vulnerable state, the enemy—the devil—wants you to give up.

The fact of the matter is that in your vulnerable state, the enemy—the devil—wants you to give up. He wants to devour you, and one of the first ways he does this is through confusion and lies. He is the father of lies (see John 8:44). He comes to steal, kill, and destroy, but Jesus came so that you might have life (see John 10:10). He—Jesus—is the way, the truth, and the life (see John 14:6), and to successfully make it through this dark valley that seems like death, you must fight. You must push through and fight the lies. You will have days when you feel like you've taken two steps forward and then four steps back, but keep pushing forward. You will have days when you don't have the strength, and that's okay. Don't think you need the strength of Samson to overcome. No. You have what you need; you have who you need. The Lord is your strength and shield; He helps you (see Psalm 28:7).

> You fight them with truth; with God's Word (see John 17:17).

"Will He still help me after...?" Yes. The Lord is faithful even when we are not. You are not alone.

"How do I fight these overwhelming and negative thoughts?" you might ask.

You fight them with truth; with God's Word (see John 17:17).

Are you ready to fight the lies?

Lie #1: "I have no reason to live on."

When I could not understand what was going on and how God allegedly broke His promise and seemingly made a fool out of me, I became depressed. I didn't want to cook food to eat. I didn't want to bathe. I didn't want to get out of my room. I just wanted to stay in my room alone in the dark, as I felt like I had no reason to live on.

You may be wrapped up in your sheets, still wearing the same clothes from last week, struggling to carry out basic daily tasks, and feeling like there is no reason to live on— no reason to live on because you feel alone, nobody cares, and anything is better than feeling this overwhelming hurt and shame. You think there is no reason to live on because what it takes to get through this is going to take so much out of you; there is no reason to live on because of all the emotional effort and/or financial resources you have already spent in preparation to marry this person. Or there is no reason to live because you feel like you have probably been mishearing the voice of God all your life.

These are all lies. Those *"No reason to live on because..."* are all lies. You have a reason to live on, despite the chaos you're going through.

When Moses was born, the pharaoh at the time ordered all male Hebrew newborns to be killed.

When Jesus was born, King Herod ordered all male babies born within the last two years to be killed.

And since you have been born, the enemy has tried many ways to abort or jeopardise your purpose—to jeopardise *"your reason to live."* But we rebuke the lies and the plans of the enemy in Jesus' name.

You.have.a.reason.to.live.

Truth #1- You have a reason to live on.

Even if you can't feel or even imagine what reason that might be, you have a purpose and a reason to live on. You will not die; instead, you will live to declare the works of the Lord and what He has done.

It is perfectly normal and okay to feel the emotions you are experiencing. Our feelings help our mind and body know what is going on. However, we must use the truth of God's Word to address lies that, in a sense, are suffocating us.

You:
- are God's handiwork and masterpiece, in Christ Jesus, created to do good works (see Ephesians 2:10).

- are chosen by God, His special possession and treasure (see 1 Peter 2:9).

God:

- began a *good* work in you and will carry it to completion (see Philippians 1:6).

- works out things for good for those who love Him and are called according to His purpose (see Romans 8:28).

- will fulfil His purpose in you and vindicate you (see Psalm 138:8).

Despite the immense pain of thinking you were going to marry someone and it not working out, there will come a time when God will wipe away every tear from your eyes. In fact, He will turn your mourning into dancing. He has good plans for you, and you must believe that, despite this storm. Jesus is in the boat with you, and you will get through, just as you have in previous times.

Lie # 2: "I can't discern God's voice in the future."

You may be questioning your relationship with God and trying to discern His voice. After all, if I got it wrong this time, then will I also be misled in the future?

I remember that after I believed God had revealed my future husband, and in the end, it did not work out, I felt like I was walking on eggshells on top of a rail of sharp blades and daggers. I feared hearing from God again. Yes, that's right, and I will repeat: *I feared hearing from God.*

I was so shaken up that I wondered if I would clearly discern God speaking to me again. I was extremely perplexed and afraid of being wrong again. So, even though I would pray and ask God to help heal and restore me, I had a hard time navigating and getting direction from God, and I was just worried about failing again.

But then I had to realize that God is a redemptive God, and I can just rest in His goodness. Even if I fail to hear or interpret correctly again in life, He is patient and will show me the way as I continue to seek His direction. He does not give His children stones when they ask for bread, and He won't give you a black hole when you seek clarity. Seek and you will find, even if it takes some time.

Truth #2: You are God's sheep, and you will hear His voice.

Have you ever been in a house or space with several people, and someone calls your name? You think it is Candice, but it turns out to be Lauren instead, or you think it was your mother, but it turns out to be your grandmother? Or maybe you knew it was your grandmother's voice, but you heard, *"Have you seen my hat?"* when, in reality, what she said was, *"Have you seen the cat?"*

I have had similar instances. Your mishearing or misinterpreting at the moment does not mean you have completely failed and are bound to mix it up again. In a physical sense, we can mishear or misinterpret for several reasons, such as noise in the background, distractions, the distance of the person speaking, or simply a misconception. Similarly, in a spiritual sense, these can impact what we hear or how we interpret what we hear.

Nevertheless, the point of the matter is that you can and will hear God's voice again in knowledge, understanding, and clarity.

You are a part of his sheepfold, and you know His voice. Yes, so and so happened, but you know His voice and will continue to listen and be guided by Him. Even if you truly don't think you know His voice, speak aloud over and over that you are His sheep, and you hear His voice.

> you can and will hear God's voice again in knowledge, understanding, and clarity.

"I am the good shepherd; I know my sheep and my sheep know me—My sheep listen to my voice; I know them, and they follow me. I give them eternal life, and they shall never perish; no one will snatch them out of my hand. My Father, who has given them to me, is greater than all; no one can

snatch them out of my Father's hand." (John 10:14, 27-29 – NIV).

You are His sheep, and no one can snatch you from the Father's hands. You know and will continue to learn to discern His voice. Pray and ask Him to give you clarity when He speaks and to remove anything that could be in the way. Moreover, most importantly, read His Word. God can speak in many ways, but what is certain is that He speaks to us and provides good wisdom in His Word for us to make decisions.

If I were truly applying the practical wisdom in God's Word, seeking wise counsel from others, and not being distracted by sin, my own expectations and ideologies, and even lust, I would have heard and interpreted things much better.

However, I was able to discern God's voice again, especially through His Word, and you will too.

You are His sheep. No one can snatch you away. Furthermore, you will hear His voice and follow Him. You will defeat the lies and walk in truth. After all, your shepherd is the way, the truth, and the life.

Lie #3: "There is no hope."

You may have found the strength to perform basic tasks and have been able to return to your daily routine. You are not as devastated as you were at first when "the one" you thought you should marry led to disappointment.
68

Nevertheless, you are still in the process of figuring out life and moving forward. You may not see any indication that things will return to normal or even better, but when you look back on this moment years later, you will see how God's grace and hope rescued you.

Truth # 3: There is hope beyond what you can even imagine.

"For I know the plans I have for you," declares the Lord, "plans to prosper you and not to harm you, plans to give you hope and a future." (Jeremiah 29:11 – NIV).

The Lord's plan for you is not one to harm and hurt you; instead, it is to prosper you and give you hope.

Jeremiah 29:11 has always been an inspiring scripture for me. Friends and fellow believers would often use it as an encouraging tool whenever I was worried about my life, a situation, or the future. They would remind me that God has a good plan for me and my future.

Nevertheless, until recently, I did not know the story and context behind this scripture. This verse is part of a larger chapter, which is a letter that Jeremiah wrote to the Israelites who were in exile. That is, the Babylonians destroyed the homes and temples of the Israelites, they were taken captive, anything of treasure and value was plundered, and persons were killed. Their lives have been completely displaced, and some of them were taken to Babylon to work in harsh conditions. They were going through a devastating period of utter pain and turmoil, and here comes a letter from the prophet Jeremiah with words from the Lord, saying, *"For I know the plans I have for you, plans to prosper you and not to harm you, plans to give you hope and a future."*

I bet some of the Israelites were like:

— *"Plans not to harm me? Pshhh! It must be the other way around."*

— *"Hope and a future? Well, nothing around me seems that way."*

— *"Plans to prosper me? Okay, if you say so."*

It must have been very difficult for the Israelites to receive this word, considering their current situation.

It must be hard for you to push forward, hold on to hope, and trust in God in your current circumstances. But remember, God is the Alpha and Omega—the beginning and the end. You may only see your present situation; nevertheless, He sees the end, and He has declared that He

> replacing those destructive thoughts and lies with the truth in God's Word in Jesus' name. Amen.

will give you hope and a future.

There might be so many other thoughts that bombard your brain throughout this process—other negative and destructive lies that aim to deprive you of moving forward. But you will move forward and be restored by replacing those destructive thoughts and lies with the truth in God's Word in Jesus' name. Amen.

Reflection

1. Make this declaration: *"I [your name] am God's handiwork. I will not die, but I will live to declare His good works."*

2. Write out three lies that are hindering your journey to restoration, and find scriptures of truth to combat them.

3. Research five qualities of God and write down the times when you saw these attributes in your walk with the Lord and your life.

Chapter 6

Acknowledge Emotions

Then he said to them, "My soul is overwhelmed with sorrow to the point of death. Stay here and keep watch with me." (Matthew 26:38 – NIV).

This was Jesus speaking about how He felt and what He was experiencing while He was in the garden of Gethsemane, right before He was arrested and then eventually crucified.

The amplified translation says, *"My soul is deeply grieved, so that I am almost dying of sorrow."*

There was a point in my Christian journey when I was not completely transparent about my emotions. I felt like a Christian should never get angry, should always be happy and joyful, and should not get anxious. However, I would always miserably fail to meet this standard. I did get angry. I was sometimes deeply sad with feelings of depression, and I battled anxiety. In essence, I would sometimes suppress my emotions and how I truly felt in order to try and live up to a standard until I realized that my emotions were not bad. They were created by God and help me to understand and regulate how I feel. They help me recognize when something is wrong so that I can address it.

It is not a case where I won't get angry; instead, when I do become angry, I should not let it cause me to sin and do bad or harmful things (see Psalm 4:4). It is not a case where I won't feel anxious or worried but whenever I do, I should cast my anxieties on the Lord because He cares for me (1 Peter 5:7). I should pray to God, give Him thanks and present my request to Him, and His peace will guard my heart.

> **you should not suppress your emotions.**

The point I am making is that you should not suppress your emotions. Be open and honest about how you feel and what you are experiencing with God. Acknowledge your emotions.

Yes, you will be fighting the lies that try to consume your mind and discourage you, but at the same time, you are being open to God about how you truly feel. Acknowledging your emotions is a key part of the process towards restoration and healing.

An inspiring story for me in the Bible has always been that of Hannah. It is short, yet it conveys a woman's pain, vulnerability, and, ultimately, her breakthrough.

Hannah was the wife of a man named Elkanah, who also had another wife named Peninnah. Peninnah had children and would constantly tease Hannah because she was barren. This would really affect Hannah emotionally to the point where Hannah would sometimes weep and not eat (see 1 Samuel 1:7).

Hannah was facing a lot. She was experiencing a range of emotions, and it was clear that it was taking a toll on her. However, she did something simple yet transformational. She poured it all out. She wept and poured out how she was really feeling and how this situation was affecting her (see 1 Samuel 1:10).

She poured out her heart to the point that, while she was at the temple weeping and pouring out her heart to God, the priest thought she was intoxicated because her lips moved but with no sound. But she was not drunk. She was laying out all her pain and anguish before God.

Similarly, there are various other references to biblical characters who were transparent and vulnerable to God about how they felt. Another prime example is King David.

King David was a strong and skilled warrior. Yet, in the Psalms, we see the strong and bold soldier vulnerably pouring out his heart and feelings to God.

When I was going through the disappointment of thinking someone was my future spouse, and it didn't turn out to be so, I felt all kinds of emotions. I went through confusion, insecurity, paranoia, panic attacks, thoughts of not wanting to be alive, anger, and bitterness.

You may be feeling a myriad of emotions, and I am here to reassure you. Pour it all out; don't bottle it in. Take a close look at how you're feeling and identify your triggers. Is there anything that triggers a certain emotion in you? Is there anything you can do to lessen your exposure to a certain emotional trigger? One of the things I had to do was block my ex's status, and eventually, I had to block him. It was an emotional trigger for me.

At the outset, we tried to remain friends; however, we would constantly argue, cause wounds, and even resurface some old ones. It was unhealthy for me. Each time I spoke to him, I would feel emotionally drained and sometimes back at square one. So I stopped talking to him. However, after that, I would still watch his status to see what was going on in his life. This also became a trigger for me. Eventually, I realized I had to let go completely and cut off all means of communication. After doing this, I realized that over time, emotionally, I would improve. I was no longer communicating with him or watching his status. I was no longer privy to information (such as his new relationship six weeks after we broke up) that caused emotional turmoil. Additionally, I had to start taking a break from social media. I would often go on Instagram and see posts of *"the perfect couple"* and videos of couples sharing *"how God wrote their love story."* At that time in my life, which would stir up some old wounds, I had to be mindful of avoiding certain emotional triggers to maintain my peace.

In this process of restoration, being honest about your emotions is essential, coupled with identifying key emotional triggers that you need to avoid. You must do what is necessary to maintain your peace and heal.

Supportive Community

As you make the necessary steps needed to become more emotionally aware and stable, you must not isolate yourself. Find community. Find support. You don't have to do this all on your own. Accept help from others.

After the prophet Elijah stood up against the prophets of Baal, called down fire from heaven, and proved that his God was the true and living God (see 1 Kings 18:16-39), Jezebel threatened to kill him. Elijah was terrified and isolated himself in the wilderness (see 1 Kings 19:1-3).

> Find community. Find support. You don't have to do this all on your own. Accept help from others.

He started having catastrophic thoughts, saying that he had had enough and God should take his life. He was feeling very downcast. His emotions were real, and isolating himself made him focus on his spiraling thoughts even more.

Do not isolate yourself. Even if you believe you are strong on your own, find community and support. Social isolation can cause you to become stuck in your own thoughts and emotions, which can impact your progress in healing. Even if you do need some time by yourself to process your emotions, ensure that you are getting the godly support you need.

One of the things that helped me significantly was getting plugged in. In my instance, I did not have a home church at the time. After the devastating situation unfolded, I found a local church home and joined a supportive small group. The support and help I received in those moments significantly helped on days when I felt like I couldn't go any further.

You were not meant to do this journey alone. Accept the help of trusted godly individuals that God has placed in your life. We are the body of Christ; we support one another. If one falls down and grows weary, the other chips in and helps, and vice versa.

Counseling and professional help are other recommended ways to find support as you navigate your emotions. Don't be held back by the stigma; it's an investment in your emotional and overall well-being. Similarly to how we visit a doctor if something feels off about the physiological aspect of our body or just for a check-up, we should also prioritize the psychological aspect. Get the wise counseling/therapy you need, as the words from the wise bring healing (see Proverbs 12:18).

Rest

As you navigate your emotions and the healing process, ensure that you rest.

In the same story of Elijah mentioned above, where he became terrified, ran away, and isolated himself, there is an interesting part of the scenario that played out. He rested. After being brutally honest with God about how he has had enough, *"he lay down under the bush and fell asleep." (1 Kings 19:5 - NIV).*

After that, an angel of the Lord woke him up, and he had something to eat. Then, he went back to sleep and rested. This reminded me of my periods of "processing," which were dedicated times in the presence of the Lord, where I would simply process my emotions and journal. Sometimes, acknowledging my emotions, identifying the triggers, surrendering how I felt to the Lord, and just everything that happened when I was "processing" took me up to three hours. When I was done, I was exhausted. I was exhausted, but my heart was usually lighter. Afterward, I would just rest, take a nap, sleep.

Now, I'm not saying you should do exactly what I did by sitting down for long, journaling, and processing.

Nevertheless, as you use whichever healthy mechanism you choose to evaluate your emotions, you must rest. Rest is essential for recuperation and rejuvenation.

> It has undergone a lot of aches and pain, so ensure that you are allowing your mind and heart to rest in God.

Allow your body to physically rest during the season. It has undergone a lot of aches and pain, so ensure that you are allowing your mind and heart to rest in God.

"Come to me, all you who are weary and burdened, and I will give you rest." (Matthew 11:28 – NIV).

Reflection

1. Journal and pour out your emotions before the Lord.

2. Research and sign up for supportive small groups or therapists that can support you on your journey.

3. Write down ways you can intentionally rest in God.

Chapter 7

Introspection

I was well on my way to fighting lies, accepting the truth, and becoming a happier person, but God kept tugging at my heart. My heart was like a specimen placed in a petri dish under a microscope, ready to be examined by God. He wanted me to introspect and, where necessary, repent.

Repent is not a word that is often used in some modern teachings. When some people think of repentance, they think of fire raining down and people hollering. Now, God's warnings of repentance can sometimes employ similar imagery. However, repentance really means to turn away from something or to change course, which I believe is paramount in your process of healing and restoration. If you stay on the same course you initially started on, it will most likely lead to continued despair. According to BibleHub.com, repentance is described as a *"change of heart and mind that leads to a turning away from sin and a turning towards God."*

In my journey to restoration and freedom, introspection and repentance have been and continue to be essential in helping me turn away from negative thought patterns and actions and turn to God. Introspection challenged certain unhealthy and sinful patterns I had, made me reflect on certain misconceptions I had about love and finding a future spouse, and resulted in me turning to God.

In essence, self-examination greatly aided me in recognizing where I went wrong in how I processed God's revelation of who "the one" was for me. Self-examination showed me how to avoid the errors I had made previously.

While writing this book, I was afraid of how stupid I would look, as readers would see some deeply rooted issues I had and some of the mistakes I made. However, I realized that my testimony could help others realize that *"they are not alone/not the only one"* and that they can get through this.

Join me as this chapter shares some of the things I learned during introspection, including some of my foolish ideologies and mistakes, and most importantly, how God's grace carried me—and will carry you too.

This was not the first time I believed God showed me who my future husband was going to be.

Sigh. Yep.

And the worst part is that I didn't consciously realize it had happened before, especially since it was so many years prior. I was only about fifteen years old at the time. Sigh again.

It's weird, as if my mind had become accustomed to processing things in a certain way, and I didn't even realize it. Thank God for His Holy Spirit, who led me to all truth and guided the process of renewing my mind. He was able to show me some of the faulty perceptions and tendencies I had and how I was predisposed to such.

I was nine years old when I got baptized. However, I made a strong commitment at the age of fourteen, thanks to great assistance and examples from a local Christian club at my high school. I was inspired by other teenagers I saw who just truly loved God. They wanted to please Him in all areas of their lives and were determined to obey His commands. It was here that I learned so much about the love of God and His Word, and it was here that God's goodness led me to true repentance. I loved the local Christian club. It was where a lot of spiritual growth occurred for me. Moreover, we would inter-fellowship with other schools and meet people in a similar age range. Nevertheless, this is where I also first heard the term, *"God showed me that he or she was going to be my future spouse."*

There was a specific girl on the leadership committee who was a little older, maybe sixteen, from whom I first heard this type of interaction. In summary, she and a guy a little older were friends and would pray with each other. One day, he asked her to pray for his future wife for him. Over time, she would pray, and eventually, through some type of confirmation from the Holy Spirit, she found that the wife was her. He was a bit older, though, probably in his early twenties, but he conveyed that he would wait for her.

"Awww, that is so cute!" is what most of the girls would say or think.

For me, I was in awe. I had always wanted to fall in love and find "the one" who would come into my life, treat me with love, and, in a sense, make my life complete.

> **"** I had always wanted to fall in love and find "the one" who would come into my life, treat me with love, and, in a sense, make my life complete. **"**

Since then, I always wondered who my future husband would be. I would often daydream—as any teenager would—about getting married and what my future life would be like.

I would meet Christian boys—I went to an all-girls high school—at various inter-fellowships, and whoever I had a crush on, I wondered, *"Could this be my future spouse?"* It was sometime during this time span that I saw someone—a little older than I—and thought he might be my future husband. But for some reason, this instance didn't go far. I was young, a new believer, and I was attending school in another part of the country. So, for some strange reason (thankfully), I forgot about him and all that.

In retrospect, I laughed because I was so young; neither was I even of legal age to get married. But I was just a teenager who wanted a "happily ever after." Now, I have no clue what happened to that girl and her *"future husband who was willing to wait on her."* She would have ended up moving to another part of the country. But I do know what happened to me; I started daydreaming so much that I idolized marriage, which I did not realize until recently.

> I started daydreaming so much that I idolized marriage, which I did not realize until recently.

Does this sound similar to you? Did you have a similar experience?

Caught-Up In Fantasies Rather Than Reality

I was a full-fledged daydreamer. I would get whisked away in fantasies and thoughts of what my future life might be, specifically my future love life. You know, the one where you drop your pen, and as you're picking it up, you lock eyes with a guy who eventually becomes the love of your life? Yup, that kind.

85

Apart from that, I absolutely loved romantic novels and romantic movies. I was always an avid reader with a huge imagination. From the time I was a little girl, whenever I read a book, it was almost as if it came alive in my head. So, whenever I read romantic novels or watch romantic movies, the story comes alive in my head so much that I create my own similar love story with a matching plot.

This followed me into adulthood. I would get so caught up in the story I created in my mind that I didn't pay as much attention to the current reality when it came to interests and relationships. Or, if I did notice something off or a red flag about reality, I would brush it off as I was eager to mold things to conform to my fantasies. It didn't help that I attended an all-girls school from the age of 13 to 18, was very introverted, and wasn't as well-versed in communicating with guys.

This was unhealthy. It led me to what I now call the *"Is he my future husband-syndrome."* This is where I would meet a guy. We started having a basic and funny conversation, and my mind would almost be like, *"Alert! Alert! Possible subject suspected. Could this be my future husband?"*

Well, not exactly like that, but my mind would wander, thinking that this could potentially be "the one." In most cases, I would start creating a story in my head about what our future would be like if and when we got married.

So, it was not surprising that when I met Bob, the same thing happened. I was already creating stories in my head of what our future life would look like. Nonetheless, there was a slight difference; eventually, he was also discussing what our future life might look like. I was head over heels; this was going to be my moment when *"God writes your love story."*

However, looking back, it was no surprise that I thought he was my "God-ordained spouse." I was already daydreaming about our future life, so it should be no surprise that I was also "night-dreaming" about it. Several of those dreams I had were likely due to the fact that I thought about this all the time during the day and before bed, so I ended up having it somewhere in my mind while asleep.

I think I was so obsessed with the story I had already created in my mind, and marriage was such a grave idol in my heart that I gave little room for God to speak to my spirit.

> I was already daydreaming about our future life, so it should be no surprise that I was also "night-dreaming" about it.

I would nevertheless pray and ask God to direct me and help me make the right decision. I would pray for His guidance to ensure I was making a good decision. However, when He spoke in practical ways, I didn't pay attention.

So I didn't pay attention when Bob and I couldn't have a Bible study together without arguing. I didn't pay attention when Bob was more of an *"isolated/by myself kind-of Christian"* and was not necessarily under authority nor a part of a local church. I didn't pay attention when he started following this international preacher who held some unusual beliefs and began adopting them. Nor did I pay attention when we first started dating, but I noticed that when we were hanging out, laughing, and talking, he would somehow position my hand to end up catching his you-know-what. Furthermore, I did not pay attention when we started having premarital sex, and when I would bawl my eyes out because of the guilt and shame *of dishonouring God.* Initially, he was *"only sad about what happened because I was sad and crying."*

I could go on and on. However, the point is that I wasn't paying attention. I was too caught up in my fantasies and made-up stories. Maybe I was looking for some bright light to shine down, after which a lion would roar, and then I would hear a voice say, *"My child, do not move forward in marriage."* That didn't happen, but what did happen was that the relationship eventually did not work out.

The Introspection

All in all, after introspecting, I realized that God was indeed *good.* At the outset, I was mad at Him and said how he had disappointed me by promising something but not coming through. But looking back now, I raise my hand in awe of how He was looking out for me. I bow my head in honor of how He saved me from what I had gotten myself into.

I realized that the fantasizing, the *"is he my future husband-syndrome,"* having marriage as an idol, and sin all combined together would have impaired my ability to hear and receive God's direction. Plus, even if I did realize what He was saying at one point, I was too caught up in the story I had already created in my mind.

During my quiet time with the Lord one day, I came across a verse: *"A person's own folly leads to their ruin, yet their heart rages against the Lord." (Proverbs 19:3 – NIV).*

This scripture convicted me deeply. I realized that my misconceptions and poor decisions had gotten me into this situation, but instead, I was angry at God—the same God who extended grace and mercy after everything, the same God who forgave me for making marriage an idol and for having premarital sex, and much more. My heavenly Father treated me like the prodigal son and waited for me to come home. My Abba Father celebrated my return and treated me no less than a son or daughter. Instead, He showered me with truth and grace.

So, I repented. I asked God to forgive me for how my heart raged against Him, and I asked that He renew my mind. I am grateful that, over time, He was able to redirect some faulty conceptions I had and provide me with truth and wisdom from His Word.

Now it's your turn.
It is your turn to be healed and renewed through introspection and repentance.

Your story might be different. Perhaps you didn't idolize marriage like I did, or often wondered if the current guy holding a small conversation with you was "the one." Or maybe you did.

However, whatever your story is, I believe it is necessary to take a step back. You must ask God to reveal and help you with any faulty misconceptions or expectations you had, and ask Him to renew your mind. Moreover, it is also essential that you repent. Turn away from any bitterness you have in your heart towards God or anyone else in this whole process. Additionally, regardless of your story, God's goodness is present, and you will see how He has protected you. You may not see it now, but you will see how He has been so faithful.

Finally, do not condemn yourself. This entire process must have been a difficult one for you, and after reading this chapter, you may feel remorseful about many things. However, remember that there is no condemnation for those who are in Christ Jesus (see Romans 8:1-2).

Yes, repentance involves sorrow for your sins, true remorse, and a willingness to turn away from that sin. However, on the other hand,

> **Allow God to restore you.**

condemnation seeks to bury you in your sin with guilt, shame, and no hope. The enemy would love for you to be drenched in condemnation and not accept the grace of God. Instead, lay it all before God, confess, repent; He will hear you.

"If we confess our sins, he is faithful and just and will forgive us our sins and purify us from all unrighteousness."
(1 John 1:9 – NIV).

Allow God to restore you.

Reflection

1. Pray a blessing for anyone in this situation with whom you may have unforgiveness or bitterness towards.

2. Read Luke 15:1-31 (The parable of the lost sheep, the lost coin, and the lost/prodigal son). Journal your thoughts.

Chapter 8

Take One Step At A Time

Don't beat yourself up if you have started implementing strategies to help you recover, but sometimes you feel like you're back to square one.

Take things one step at a time.

One day, I was on social media; if I remember correctly, it was during the week of Valentine's Day. I was scrolling, and then a random reel appeared of a couple talking about their love story and how God brought them together. You could see the deep affection between them. Out of nowhere, I just started bawling. In the midst of my crying, I started quickly drying my tears, saying, *"No, Lori! You're over this already. Stop it!"*

I tried to talk myself out of crying, but the tears continued to stream down my cheeks nonetheless.

"For I am the Lord your God who takes hold of your right hand and says to you, Do not fear; I will help you." (Isaiah 41:13 – NIV).

> 66
> Do not beat yourself up. This is a journey, not necessarily just a destination.
> 99

You may find yourself in a circumstance where you feel like you should have progressed further in the healing process; certain things should not bother you anymore. You are going about your merry business when something unexpectedly triggers an emotional response or brings back hurtful memories.

Do not beat yourself up. This is a journey, not necessarily just a destination. The Lord is with you, helping you every step of the way.

You feel like you would have retracted instead of progressing. Perhaps you've found yourself having spiraling negative thoughts again. Perhaps you have been trying to fight off some lies you thought would have been defeated by now. Maybe you still feel down when memories come back to your mind. And perhaps you're being too hard on yourself.

Remember that restoration is a process.

There were moments when I fell back into negative thoughts and questioned the possibility of hope—hope to truly heal from this trauma, hope to trust God again, or even just hope regarding relationships in the future.

Throughout this process, I have learned—and am still learning—that it takes one step at a time. You may see five flights of stairs before you to climb, and it looks impossible, but with every single step, you are closer to the top. With every single step, you are closer to the end result. Yes, you may have to pause sometimes to catch your breath. Maybe at some point, you had to lean on the rail for support or perhaps even just pause on a specific step until you gathered the strength and motivation to move up the next few steps. The average person doesn't just take three gigantic steps, and bam, they have climbed a few flights of stairs in two seconds. Of course not. It takes time.

You may still be "climbing your stairs" of overcoming the shame of being wrong about who you thought your future husband was going to be. Maybe you still see people who you told, *"That is my future husband."* So now you wonder if they are looking at you weird or laughing behind your back.

One step at a time.

You may still be "climbing your stairs" of letting go of all bitterness and anger (see Ephesians 4:31) as you watch who you thought was your future spouse get married to someone else, and it's a big celebration.

One step at a time.

You may be "climbing your stairs" of disappointment as the man you are sure is to be your future spouse has never spoken to you or shown any interest. It has been years, and you have been faithfully waiting.

> He is a light to your path, and His Word is a lamp for your feet (see Psalm 119:105).

One step at a time.

Remember, the Lord holds your right hand, and He will help you. He is a light to your path, and His Word is a lamp for your feet (see Psalm 119:105).

Patience

Something I am currently learning on my walk with the Lord is patience. Throughout my walk with the Lord, as I developed my character and the fruit of the Spirit, I thought that, for the most part, I was patient.

Nevertheless, recently, the Holy Spirit has been convicting me of being impatient when it comes to the future. Sometimes I get so caught up in wanting to know what the future holds and what lies ahead that my impatience causes me to become anxious. The truth is, based on my past experiences, I am afraid of failing again. Based on my past experiences, I sometimes fear what the future holds. So, I bombard my brain with numerous possible ideas and how I plan to tackle them if this or that happens, because I am afraid of failing.

However, the Lord is teaching me patience, and the truth is that even if I did know everything about the future and planned accordingly, I would still need Jesus. Even if I knew that there would be a couple of bumps in six months and a huge rock in three years, I would still need Jesus there with me every step of the way.

I am saying all of this to encourage you to be patient and take it one step at a time. Be grateful for the strides you have already made and focus on tackling the course right in front of you rather than becoming too perplexed and worried about the future.

Moreover, avoid comparing yourself and your progress to anyone around you. Instead, *"Let your eyes look straight ahead; fix your gaze directly before you. Give careful thought to the paths for your feet and be steadfast in all your ways." (Proverbs 4:25-26 - NIV).*

God's Strength

This journey is not one that can be accomplished alone. It was previously mentioned that you need to find a support system of godly people and explore counseling on this path.

Nevertheless, relying on God's strength is more important than anything. Trust me, take it from me: I have tried many times to figure everything out and do it all in my own strength, which only leads to exhaustion and frustration.

However, when I allow the Holy Spirit to step in and help strengthen me, oh, what a difference.

As you embark on this path of healing and taking things one step at a time, remember:

- The Lord is your strength and your shield; He helps you (see Psalm 28:7).

- It is not by might nor by power, but by God's Spirit (see Zechariah 4:6).

- His grace is sufficient for you, and His strength is made perfect in your weakness (see 2 Corinthians 12:9).

- He is your refuge, a very present help in times of trouble (see Psalm 46:1).

- He will be with you as you pass through the floods and rivers that seem like they will overwhelm you (see Isaiah 43:2).

- He comforts you, even though you walk through the valley of the shadow of death (see Psalm 23:4).

Allow God's strength to take you through as you take things one step at a time.

Reflection

1. Write down three areas where you have seen at least some form of improvement throughout this journey.

2. Write ten things you are grateful for in life.

Chapter 9

Hopefulness

"May the God of hope fill you with all joy and peace as you trust in him, so that you may overflow with hope by the power of the Holy Spirit." (Romans 15:13 – NIV).

God has a way of transforming a hopeless and dim situation into one that is hopeful and filled with light. The entire story of salvation in the Bible, as told through Jesus Christ, displays this, and in your life story, you will also see His hope. It is in His nature; He is the God of hope.

Looking back on when I first started this journey and where I am now, I can see God's goodness, and I am hopeful for the future. As you walk this journey of rebuilding trust in God and deepening

> God has a way of transforming a hopeless and dim situation into one that is hopeful and filled with light.

your relationship with Him, remain hopeful. Your hope is

not that everything will become perfect instantly, and you will have all the answers. Instead, your hope is in the one who perfects everything concerning you and knows the end from the beginning.

My prayer for everyone who reads this book is that He will continually fill you with hope. I pray that you will overflow with joy, peace, and all the blessings that come from the Lord, and that His Holy Spirit will guide you. My prayer is that the Lord will do in your life more than you could ever ask or think as you put your hope in Him.

There will be days when you don't fully understand, feel discouraged, and want to throw in the towel. Nevertheless, the God of hope is your anchor.

"Is there truly hope?" You may be wondering.

It's okay to wonder, especially if what is immediately in front of you seems disheartening instead of hopeful. Nevertheless, the God of hope can turn the most discouraging situation into one of hope.

If anyone knows what it is like to lose hope, it is Joseph (see Genesis 37, 39-47).

A young man with a lot of dreams and goals for the future, Joseph was only seventeen when his life took a devastating turn. His brothers, out of envy and anger towards him, attacked him, ripped off his clothes, and threw him into a pit to eventually die. But if that was not bad enough, they decided to sell him as a slave, where he was taken to a foreign land. His brothers did not just strip him of his clothes and dignity that day; they stripped him of his home, family, identity, and security. I can hardly imagine the pain Joseph must have felt on that journey to Egypt. One minute, he was around his father, who loved him so much, free and taken care of, and the next minute, he was a slave who lost touch with everything and everyone he knew before. Joseph, however, didn't lose touch with God.

Joseph eventually became a servant to an Egyptian official, and things started looking hopeful. He worked hard, was trusted by his master, and was able to govern all of his master's affairs. Nevertheless, hope was stripped from him, and life became worse than it had been before. His master's wife lied that he was trying to forcefully sleep with her, and he was thrown into prison. What a tragedy! From a young man with many dreams and hopes to a slave to a falsely accused criminal.

Hopelessness is the perfect word to describe how Joseph's situation seemed. He is now a foreign slave who has become a prisoner. He has no one and no family in the country to look out for him or speak on his behalf. Once again, it was as if he were left to die and to be forgotten.

Nevertheless, there is something about the God of hope. Joseph went from being a slave and a prisoner to being second in command to Pharaoh as his advisor.

Being disappointed about who you should marry after you truly believed God had revealed it to you can definitely feel like being in a desolate, foreign land where it becomes hard to trust God again and remain hopeful. But the God of hope is in the midst. Similarly, you will see hope and restoration in your life as you walk through the process of rebuilding trust in God.

Hope in God's Promises

God's promises are "yes and amen" (see 2 Corinthians 1:20), and as you tread this journey towards restoration, remind yourself of His promises. Once again, I draw on the reference from Jeremiah 29:11: *"For I know the plans I have for you," declares the Lord, "plans to prosper you and not to harm you, plans to give you hope and a future." (NIV).* Similarly to the Israelites who were going into slavery and exile when they received this word, you might not see how this truly applies to you based on what you are currently experiencing. However, believe with all your heart that there is hope. Believe with all your heart and hope in God's promises through faith, which *"is confidence in what we hope for and assurance about what we do not see." (Hebrews 11:1 - NIV).*

Be reminded of God's promises:

104

- He heals the broken-hearted and binds up their wounds (see Psalm 147:3).

- You have hope; because of God's love, you are not consumed. His compassion and loving-kindness is new every morning (see Lamentations 3:21-23).
- The Lord is good to those whose hope is in Him, to the one who seeks Him (see Lamentations 3:25).

- Those who hope in the Lord will renew their strength (see Isaiah 40:31).

- The Lord is your refuge and shield; put your hope in the Word (see Psalm 119:114).

- Even when you walk through the darkest valley, you will not fear. His rod and staff comfort you (see Psalm 23:4).

- He is surely with you always, to the very end of the age (see Matthew 28:20).

Hope For The Future

Throughout my healing journey, I have come a long way. I would have processed a lot of my emotions, engaged in a lot of introspection, and continuously tried to remain hopeful in God and His promises. However, there was still something lingering for which I wondered if I would have hope again concerning *that thing.* That thing was relationships.

Hidden in my heart throughout this whole process was the belief that, yes, God could restore me and give me hope, but perhaps not in future relationships. I often thought about how I had messed up in my previous relationship.

"Yeah, God will provide hope, but maybe I will not get another chance concerning a relationship," I thought.

Nevertheless, God is the God of hope. Even after my experience, I have been single for a few years, and I am hoping in God in all things.

You may have doubts about the future, particularly in terms of navigating this situation, regaining your trust in God, rebuilding your confidence and identity, or even questioning future relationships. However, *"May the God of hope fill you with all joy and peace as you trust in him, so that you may overflow with hope by the power of the Holy Spirit."* *(Romans 15:13- NIV).*

Reflection

1. Write down three reasons why you will continue to hope in God.

Chapter 10

Final Thoughts

This has definitely been a rocky but rewarding journey. As I reflect on my story, I'm reminded that it is not about the pain or the heartbreak; it's about redemption, restoration, and hope. It's about how I have received a crown of beauty for ashes. It's about the God who has been faithful, even when I couldn't see it. It's about the journey of discovery, growth, and transformation that has brought me to this place.

As I look back on the journey that has brought me to this place, I'm reminded of the countless moments when I felt lost and alone. The moments when the pain of heartbreak seemed unbearable, and the questions I had about God's goodness and sovereignty threatened to consume me. But in the midst of the chaos, I discovered a profound truth: God's love, grace, truth, kindness, and plans are not limited by our circumstances.

In the darkest moments, when it seemed like all hope was lost, God was working behind the scenes, orchestrating every detail to bring me to this moment—this moment where I can look back and see the beauty of restoration, the power of forgiveness, and the transformative nature of hope.

My story is not unique. You may have walked through similar experiences, wondering if God has abandoned you or if you've misinterpreted His plans. But I want to assure you that you are not alone. Your story, though marked by pain and heartbreak, is part of a larger narrative—one of redemption, restoration, and hope.

As I've shared my journey with you, I hope you've seen that restoration is not a destination; it's a process. It's a journey of fighting lies, acknowledging emotions, introspecting, taking small steps, and finding hope in God. It's a journey that requires patience, trust, and surrender.

Despite every moment of pain, every tear shed, and every question asked, there is hope. Hope that God is good, even when our circumstances are not. Hope that God's plans are better than ours, even when we can't see the bigger picture. Hope that God's love is sufficient, even when we feel unlovable. Hope that He will strengthen us because we cannot do this journey alone.

As you close this book, I want to leave you with a challenge. Don't give up hope. Don't lose faith. Don't let the pain of your past define your future. Instead, choose to trust God, even when it's hard. Choose to believe that He is good and that He has a plan to prosper you, not to harm you.

I hope that my story has inspired you to hold onto hope, even when it seems impossible. I hope that you have been reminded that you're not alone, that you're part of a community of believers who have walked through similar experiences and have emerged stronger on the other side.

As you look to the future, I pray that you will hold onto hope, trust in God, and believe that He has a plan to give you a future and a hope.

May you overflow with hope, dear reader. May you trust God, even when it's hard. And may you believe that He has a plan to give you a future and a hope.

Reflection

1. What have you learned through this process of rebuilding trust in God and receiving healing and restoration?

If you need further support on this journey, please don't hesitate to reach out to me.

Connect with me via my website at https://lorikayemyles.com, and check out free resources, including devotionals and infographics, to help you on this journey.

Notes

1. "Good" (n.d.).merriam-webster.com Retrieved (January 2, 2025) from https://kingjamesbibledictionary.com/Dictionary/repe nt

2. "Sovereign" (n.d.). dictionary.com Retrieved (January 4, 2025) from https://www.dictionary.com/browse/sovereign

3. "Repent" (n.d.). kngjamesbibledictionary.com Retrieved (January 6, 2025) from https://kingjamesbibledictionary.com/Dictionary/repe nt

4. "Repent" (n.d.). biblehub.com Retrieved (January 6, 2025) from https://biblehub.com/topical/r/repent.htm

5. Jarrett, Ed. "How Do We Reconcile God's Sovereignty and Human Free Will? - Topical Studies." Bible Study Tools, 16 Sept. 2020, www.biblestudytools.com/bible-study/topical-studies/how-do-we-reconcile-gods-sovereignty-and-human-free-will.html.

About The Author

Lori-Kaye Myles is a devoted daughter of God and disciple of Christ, passionately committed to sharing God's love and encouraging others on their journey of faith. As a commissioned street pastor, Lori-Kaye is dedicated to spreading God's good news of salvation and His love.

Her personal journey of faith has been marked by moments of profound joy, deep sorrow, and trust. A pivotal moment came when Lori-Kaye believed God revealed her future husband to her. However, as time unfolded, unexpected disappointment tested her faith and trust in God. This experience, though challenging, fueled her desire to support others in rebuilding hope and trust in God despite their own disappointments in life or relationships.

Through her writing and ministry, Lori-Kaye invites others to join her on a journey of faith, vulnerability, and uncertainty. With transparency and humility, she shares her own struggles and triumphs, offering a message of hope and redemption. Lori-Kaye's heart beats for those who have felt disappointed, disillusioned, or disconnected from God. She longs to help them rediscover trust in God's goodness and sovereignty. Lori-Kaye's ministry is built on the foundation of her faith, which holds that God's desire is to be in a relationship with His children through salvation in Christ Jesus. She believes that by sharing our stories, vulnerabilities, and struggles, we can create a safe space for others to do the same, ultimately drawing closer to God and one another.

Through her book, "God, Was I Wrong?", Lori-Kaye offers a powerful exploration of trust, faith, and relationships. Join her on this journey of discovery as she invites you to confront your own doubts, fears, and uncertainties whilst rediscovering the goodness and love of God.